IF I SHOULD STEP ON YOUR TOES...

Just Say Ouch!

Books by Pierre D. Perry

The Voice Of Blackness

Brown Eyed Vision: Life Through The Eyes of a Black Man

Let's Talk Love: Poems of Love, Joy, & Pain

If Not Me, Who?

From The Heart of a Man

Heaven Is My Destination: Poetry for the Heart, Soul, and Mind

If I Should Step On Your Toes...Just Say Ouch!

IF I SHOULD STEP ON YOUR TOES...

Just Say Ouch!

Poems

Pierre D. Perry

PDP Publishing

Henderson, North Carolina

First Printing

TM

PDP
Publishing
is a trademark design belonging to Pierre D. Perry and PDP Publishing (USA).

"A Pierre D. Perry Book"

ISBN 13: 978-0-6156-5558-1 (paperback edition)
ISBN 10: 0-6156-5558-0
Published by PDP Publishing
Henderson, North Carolina 27536

Printed in the United States of America

ACKNOWLEDGMENTS

I would like to thank PDP Publishing for their support and willingness to take a chance on my work. Thanks for allowing my voice to be heard.

Thanks to my family for their continued support of my work. I would especially like to thank my mother for continuing to believe in me.

Thanks to my daughters (Cierra & Kenya) for continuing to make me proud. It is that pride given to me by them that makes me be the best I can be.

Thanks to Catherine Jackson for her loyalty as a friend. (Thanks for having my back)

Thanks to my father (Mr. James F. Perry) for teaching me what it means to work hard and not to expect a hand-out (work for what you want!)

Thanks to my St. Paul Presbyterian Church family for their continued support.

Last, but not least, I would like to thank God for all of the many blessings He has bestowed upon me.

*This book is
dedicated to everyone
whose toes I stepped
on
(ouch!)*

CONTENTS

PART 3: KEEP RISING!

PART 4: LIFE...IT AIN'T ALL ROSES

PART 5: PRESSURE, PRIDE, AND PAIN

A MESSAGE FROM THE AUTHOR

Greetings to all and glory be to God. First, I would like to thank you for taking time out to read my book. I hope you enjoy reading it as much as I enjoyed writing it. I've said this before and I will say it again: "My poetry is my voice, and writing poetry is my way of letting my voice be heard. My poetry has been known to step on the toes of some people, and I make no apologies about it. I don't mean to sound cocky or arrogant, because I am not. But what I am is truthful about the way I feel about certain issues. And if you find that to be offensive, I would suggest you not read my work. I realize that I will not be a favorite amongst everyone. I don't write for fame or glory, nor do I write to please everyone. I write to shine a light on dark issues that some people like to pretend doesn't exist. We would all like to think that we live in a perfect world, but we all know that don't exist. Because the world that I live in still have young black men being shot and killed for no reason at all, other than just being a black male. The world in which I live in still tries to show me that I am not equal to others of a different race. The world that I live in still tries to make me believe that even if a man of color rises to the top and holds the highest office this country has to give, he is still not as good as his white brothers. The world in which I live in would rather worry about what's on the moon than to fix the problems we have right here on earth. The world in which I live in is more concerned about money than the well being of the people. Yes, I know my poetry is offensive to some people, but that's alright, I am offended everyday of my life by some of the things that I have to encounter. So, all I can say is: "If I should step on your toes... just say ouch!.

Pierre D. Perry

PART 1

TRUE COLORS

TRUE COLORS

IF I SHOULD STEP ON YOUR TOES

If I should step on your toes
with what I have to say,
just say "ouch!"
and get-the-hell out of my way!

I'm gonna speak my mind,
because that's who I am.
And if you don't like it,
I don't giva damn!

I say what needs to be said,
from the truth I don't run.
I refuse to be quiet
until I am done.

When dealing with me,
you must have thick skin.
If I have something to say,
I will not keep it in.

I'm not one to sugar-coat
anything I have to say.
I give it to you straight!
That's just my way.

So, if I should step on your toes,
and make you angry or mad,
all I can say is...
"That's too damn bad!"

17

I COME IN PEACE

I bring no hatred with me
into this world of inequality.
But I do bring a strong determination
to rectify the problem.

I refuse to sit back
and accept the unacceptable.
I refuse to turn a blind eye
to unjust and evil ways.

I come in peace,
but I will shed blood.
I bring harm to no one,
as long as no harm comes to me.

I refuse to turn the other cheek,
only to be smacked on that one, too.
I'm always looking up,
even though you prefer my head bowed.

I start no fights,
but I will fight back.
I would love to love everyone,
but I realize everyone is not lovable.

I bring no hatred with me
into this world of inequality.
I come in peace,
but I will shed blood.

CLEAN CUT CRIMINAL

Help! Help!
Police! Police!
Help! We've been robbed!
Please, somebody help!

Yes officer, he tricked us
into helping him get in.
Therefore, we did all we could
to help him get in that white house.

He was very clean-cut,
and nicely dressed.
He looked as if
he had just left church service.

A real smooth talker
that said all the right things.
He made false promises
he had no intentions delivering on.

Once he got in,
he robbed us blind.
Left us feeling foolish
and angry for trusting him.

Who was he, you ask?
Someone more dangerous than any street thug.
Yes, he was one of them...
just another lying-ass politician!

COLOR BLIND

If I said I didn't see color,
  I would be telling a bold face lie.
If it's Okay for them to see color,
  why can't I?

It sounds good when people say,
  color doesn't matter.
But as a black man in America,
  that's just a bunch of chit-chatter.

Yeah, things have changed,
  and we have come a long way.
But I am reminded that I'm a black man
  every single day.

I refuse to believe the lie
  that America is color blind.
For me to believe that lie,
  I would have to be outta my damn mind.

I'm proud of who I am,
  and the color of my skin.
But before anyone tries to judge me,
  they should get to know the person within.

No, we shouldn't ignore race
  by pretending to be color blind.
But instead of just opening our eyes,
  we should also open our minds.

AMERICA'S TRUE COLORS

If President Barack Obama
didn't do anything else as president,
he sure did make the American people
reveal their true colors:

Red, White & Blue

red-neck,
white folks,
feeling blue...
about having a black president.

TELEVISED KKK MEETING

Today is January 15, 2012,
the 83rd birthday of Dr. Martin Luther King, Jr.,
and there is a KKK meeting
on television.
They seem to be debating over
who's going to be the next "grand wizard."

Oh no, please forgive me!
That's not a KKK meeting,
it's the 2012, Republican presidential debate.

(I guess they are both one in the same)

BLACK HISTORY MONTH

Why is it that in February,
we black people become so black,
and then as soon as March 1st comes,
we give it all back?

We are so black and proud
for twenty-eight days.
Afterward, we go right back
to our "lily-white" ways.

We can't just have pride
for that short time frame.
If so, we are allowing ourselves
to be tricked by their game.

There's a reason why we were allowed
the shortest month of the year.
Too much "black pride" and "black unity"
is the white man's fear.

They don't want the truth about "black history"
to correctly be told.
Because that means the truth about "white history"
would have to unfold.

We are a proud race of people
with a lot to celebrate and cheer.
So let's take pride in our history
everyday of the year.

WHAT IF?

What if
there was justice for all?
What if
all men were treated as equals?
What if
race really didn't matter in America?
What if
we did all love thy neighbor?
What if
politicians really did speak the truth?
What if
everyone was given a fair chance?
What if
drugs weren't a target for the "black community"?
What if
people really did believe in one race (the human race)?
What if
AIDS had never been invented for certain people?
What if
the government wasn't ran by crooks?
What if
this land had never been stolen from the Native Americans?
What if
Christopher Columbus really had discovered America?
What if
there never had to be a civil war?
What if
Christians really did practice what they preach?
What if
America really was what it stands for? (hmm!)

MY BLACKNESS

My blackness is not something
that I am ashamed of.
I see my blackness as a blessing
from the heavens above.

My blackness is my source
of strong motivation.
My proud, rich heritage
gives me great inspiration.

My blackness is something
that I truly embrace.
I refuse to be handicapped
by color or race.

I will not be left out
due to the color of my skin.
My strong sense of pride
makes me determined to get in.

My blackness empowers me
to keep my head held high.
My blackness gives me the courage
to look the devil in the eye.

My blackness gives me the strength
to be the best I can be.
In my opinion, "My Blackness"
is the best part of me!

PART 2

FREEDOM, JUSTICE, AND EQUALITY

IF I COULD FLY AWAY

If I could fly away,
I would fly to a place where I could be free...

Free to be ME!
Free to be HAPPY!
Free to be RESPECTED!
Free to be EQUAL!

Just imagine... A happy, respected me, who is treated as an equal.

If I could fly away,
I would fly to a place where I could be free...

Free to be MYSELF!
Free to be AT PEACE!
Free to be LOVED!
Free to be APPRECIATED!

Just imagine... Me, being at peace with myself all because I am loved and appreciated.

If I could fly away, I would fly away.
But since I can't, I guess I'll stay right here and fight to be free.

THE "OBAMA" FACTOR

When Barack Obama became the first black
president of the United States of America,
he made more than just history.
He made lives change forever.

Because of President Barack Obama,
black children can now believe "the sky is the limit."
And they can reach for it
knowing that it is within their grasp.

Because of President Barack Obama,
the phrase "You can be anything you want to be"
now has new meaning for children of color.
Because they now have proof to the fact.

Because of President Barack Obama,
little black boys can now desire to be more
than just a rapper, drug dealer, gangsta,
or an athlete of some kind.

Because of President Barack Obama,
not only can black children believe in "The Dream,"
but now they can began to have dreams of their own,
and know that their dreams can come true.

Because of President Barack Obama,
black children have been given new hope.
And even though the playing field is still not even,
at least they know they can have some say in their outcome.

FREEDOM AIN'T FREE!

Freedom ain't free!
Many people died for you and me!

Many black people were humiliated, shamed,
and caused a lot of disgrace;
all because they desired to be a part of the human race.

Hell no! Freedom damn sure ain't free!

Equality ain't free!
Many people died for you and me.

Many black people were kicked, beaten, spat on,
and even killed in the middle of the night;
just for marching and protesting for their own equal rights.

Hell no! Equality damn sure ain't free!

Justice ain't free!
Many people died for you and me!

Many black people have been mistreated,
abused, and falsely accused;
due to a justice system that is often misused.

Hell no! Justice damn sure ain't free!

If you believe that "Freedom" is free, you are "Freedumb".
Because you wold have to be dumb to think "Freedom" is
free.

WAIT!

Wait!
They say:
Wait for freedom!
Wait for justice!
Wait for equality!
...soon it shall come.

How long should we wait?

Should we wait like a kid on Christmas eve,
waiting for Santa to come?

Should we wait like a farmer waiting on rain,
so that he can produce a good crop?

Should we wait like someone who is stranded on a
deserted island waiting to be rescued?

Soon "wait" becomes "weight" which is a very heavy load.
And we all know that "weight" broke the wagon.
Therefore, we can not "wait" any longer.

SPEAK BLACK MAN!

Speak black man!
Be silent no more!
You've listened long enough.
Now it's your time to roar!

Speak black man!
Let them know how you feel!
Say what's on your mind!
Let them know you are for real!

Speak black man!
Don't hold anything back!
Get it all off your chest!
Don't giv'em any slack!

Speak black man!
Let them know what you are about!
When it's all said and done,
leave them without any doubt!

Speak black man!
To yourself be true!
Speak loudly! Speak proudly!
Speak up for you!

Speak black man!
Let your voice be heard!
For once in your life,
you have the last word!

PEACE, LOVE, AND UNITY

Whatever happened to the love
in the black community?
Whatever happened to the peace
and the strong unity?

Now-a-days it seems like
we have no love for each other.
We no longer giva damn about
our sister or brother.

We don't have each other back
like we did back in the day.
Instead of coming together,
we've gone the other way.

Black on black crime
is at an all time high.
Black men are killing each other,
and they don't know why.

Selfishness and greed
have taken over our hearts.
And just like sharp razors,
they have split us apart.

We talk a good game
about peace, love, and unity.
But I really don't see it
in the black community.

LET ME OUT!

Let me out of this world
that's not even mine!
Let me out of this life
that I can't define!

Let me out of this place
that is causing me pain!
Let me out this situation
that is driving me insane!

Let me out! Let me out!
I can't take anymore!
I feel like I'm stranded at sea,
and I'm ready to come ashore.

Let me out! Let me out!
The walls are closing in!
Let me out of this world
that is so full of sin!

Let me out of this place
that is fueled by hate!
Let me out of this hell,
before it's too late!

Let me out! Let me out!
You heard what I said!
Before I stay here any longer,
I would rather be dead!

THE SKIN I'M IN (for Trayvon Martin)

How can I be comfortable
with the skin I'm in,
when there are people who are allowed
to freely kill black men?

Just because of my skin color,
I gets no respect!
And because I am a black man,
I'm always a suspect!

I'm not allowed to walk
in a white neighborhood.
And if I do, I'm considered
to be up to no good.

I can get shot and killed,
and the police doesn't care.
They'll just say,
I had no business there.

And I'm supposed to be a man
filled with black pride?
But in certain neighborhoods
I have to run and hide.

Well, I don't think so!
It doesn't matter how the devil tries to attack,
Because, dead or alive,
I'm still proud to be black!

TIRED SHOULDERS

Sometimes I feel like I have the weight of the world on my
shoulders.
Other people's burdens are weighing me down like heavy
boulders.

I'm tired of having to live up to the expectations of others!
I'm tired of having to prove myself to my white brothers!

I'm tired of the fake smiles on their fake faces!
I'm tired of the fearful looks when I enter places!
I'm tired of being stereotyped by other races!

Yes, my shoulders are tired, but I'm getting stronger!
And I refuse to be held down any longer!

I'm tired of being judged by the color of my skin!
I'm tired of being made to feel less than other men!
I'm tired of people not knowing the person within!

I'm tired of being unjustly and falsely accused!
I'm tired of being mentally and physically abused!
I'm tired of being disrespected and so often misused!

Yes, my shoulders are tired of this excess weight!
All brought upon me due to others' hate.

But, just because I'm tired, it doesn't mean I'll quit.
I'm just here to let them know "I'm tired of this shit!"

PART 3

KEEP RISING!

RULES OF THE GAME

Don't believe everything that you are told
Don't buy everything that's being sold
Don't chase after every pot of gold
...take this advice and live to grow old!

Don't try to fit in where you don't belong
Don't be weak when it's time to be strong
Don't do something that you know is wrong
...go against this advice and you will die young!

Don't be afraid to stand on your own
Don't be afraid to face the unknown
Don't let your fear of the enemy be shown
...now take this knowledge and pass it on!

DREAM KILLERS

Dream killers,
they try very hard to keep you down.
The smiles on their faces
come from your frown.

They go against everything
you strive to achieve.
To make you think you are a failure
is what they want you to believe.

Their only desire
is to cause you pain.
Their pleasure comes from
turning your sunshine into rain.

Dream killers will sometime
masquerade in the form of a friend.
But their only goal is to bring
your happiness to an end.

They can also be
family members, too.
They will use every opportunity
to get close to you.

Dream killers are just that...
killers of dreams.
So always be aware
of who's on your team.

KEEP RISING!

To my brothas and sistas
who are proud to be black,
it's time to step up to the plate,
and no longer be held back!

We've been at the bottom
for too damn long!
No more singing the blues,
we're writing a new song!

We've got to fight to win!
We can't take our eyes off the prize!
Just like the temperature in July,
it's now time to rise!

We must stay strong,
for there is no time to be weak.
We must keep on rising
until we reach our peak.

We're going full speed ahead,
we can't dare stop!
Keep rising my people!
We're going to the top!

Come one! Come all!
Come one million strong!
It's time to take our place
right where we belong (at the top!)

No more shaking or faking,
or living in fear.
It's time to let them know
that we are here!

Keep rising!
Just like the sun.
Let your light shine bright!
We are second to none.

Keep rising!
Just like an elevator.
Keep moving on up
right past the hater.

Keep rising!
Stay at the bottom no more!
Press the button,
and on to the top floor.

Keep rising!
Until we reach our goal.
Keep rising!
It's time we take control.

Keep rising!
Just like the price of gas.
And if they don't like it,
tell'em to kiss your ass!

THE BLAME GAME

Listen up black people,
while I step on your toes.
This might just hurt
like a punch in the nose.
But right is right,
and wrong is wrong.
So let's put some blame
right where it belongs.
We've got to stop always
blaming "the white man",
when we ourselves are not doing
all that we can.
We must teach our children
the difference between right and wrong.
We must educate our children
to help them become mentally strong.
We must set the example
by leading the way.
We must ensure that our children
have a brighter day.
We need to quit worrying about
the latest name brand.
And worry more about putting
books in our children hands.
It's time we stop our kids
from all this misbehaving.
And from their time of birth,
we should start a college savings.
We should be at the schools
hearing what the teachers have to say.

We should be more involved
in our school's PTA.
It's time we really get it together,
and have our children backs.
It's time we ensure that our children
stay on the right track.
You must ask yourself:
Am I doing all that I can do?
Because when you point your finger,
there's three pointing back at you.

PUT THE GUN DOWN!

Put the gun down!
Go ahead and put it away!
Come on black man,
today is a new day!

You are more than just a thug,
or some dumb-ass nigger!
You wasn't born a killer,
so take your finger off the trigger!

Put the gun down!
No need for robbing and stealing.
I know that you are hurting,
but now is the time for some healing.

That gun doesn't bring respect,
it only brings fear.
And if you pull that trigger,
your problems won't disappear.

Too many black lives have been lost
while playing the "tough guy" game.
Now use your head,
and don't you dare do the same.

Put the gun down!
That's not all that you can do!
It's time to show the world
there's a lot more to you!

A "THANK YOU" TO REAL BLACK MEN

"Thank you" to the real black men
who are doing what they are supposed to do.
And if you are one of those black men,
this "Thank you" is to you.

Thank you for being a role model,
and a leader in our community.
Thank you for committing yourself
to peace, love, and unity.

Thank you for setting examples
for our young people to see.
Thank you for showing our young boys
how a real man should be.

Thank you for giving our black women
their deserving love and respect.
Thank you for giving our daughters
an idea of what they should expect.

Thank you for taking the time
to volunteer to help another.
Thank you for being someone
who is a keeper of his brother.

Thank you for being the type of man
our community needs to see.
Thank you for being "The Man"
you are supposed to be.

TO MY YOUNG SISTA

To my young sista
trying to find her way,
keep faith in God,
and know there is a better day.

Know that you are beautiful,
inside and out.
Regardless of what others say,
never have self-doubt.

Pay no attention to the negativity.
Don't let it cause you stress.
Know that you are "Somebody!"
And never think anything less.

Always take great pride
in all that you do.
Always be honest, loyal,
and to yourself be true.

Keep your head held high,
and never walk in shame.
We all make mistakes,
but that's just part of the game.

Never forget to be a lady,
and demand your respect.
And just keep in mind...
God ain't done with you yet.

TO MY YOUNG BROTHA

To my young brotha
who is lost and confused,
you must stop allowing yourself
to be misguided and misused.

Be your own man,
and lead your own way.
Stop worrying about
what "the boys" have to say.

To be a man,
you will have to stand on your own.
And sometimes that means
you will have to stand alone.

Always stay positive,
and stay on the right track.
Don't worry about the negativity,
because God has your back.

Love yourself,
and keep your self-respect.
Don't do something stupid
that you will later regret.

Remember this message
to always be true.
You come from great people,
so there must be greatness in you.

UNSTOPPABLE

In my lifetime,
I have so much to achieve.
And no one is going to stop me,
because in God, I believe!

I am unstoppable!
I aim not to lose!
Whatever I wanna be
is whatever I choose.

If it's a game to win,
I will not be beat!
When you go against me,
prepare to face defeat.

It's full speed ahead!
I will not stop!
If it's a mountain to climb,
I'm reaching the top!

I am unstoppable!
I refuse to be denied!
I face all fears,
because I'm too proud to hide.

If it's a race to run,
I'm taking first place.
If you're looking for a champion,
look for my face!

MOUNTAIN, GET OUT OF MY WAY!

I am but a man,
striving to be the best.
I aim to be number one,
and to hell with the rest.

I'm running over the big dogs!
I'm leading the pack!
I'm giving it all I've got,
and I'm not looking back!

I'm following my heart,
and I will not be led astray.
I'm going full steam ahead!
So mountain, get out of my way!

The sky is the limit
to what I can achieve.
I refuse to allow others
to tell me what to believe.

I'm not going left,
when I know to go right.
I'm coming out of the darkness,
and into the light.

I am but a man,
but giants I will slay.
I'm gonna achieve my goal!
So mountain, get out of my way!

I've taken off the blinders,
and now I can clearly see.
There is a bright future
right in front of me.

I will not be held down!
I will not be held back!
I'm giving hell to the devil
before he gets me off track.

I'm gonna live my dream!
I'm gonna have my day!
Nothing is going to stop me!
So mountain, get out of my way!

PART 4

LIFE...IT AIN'T ALL ROSES

TODAY, I...

Today, I...
Today, I did the unbearable.
Today, I did something
I had hoped to never have to do.
Today, I did the unthinkable.
The hardest thing I have ever had to do in my life,
I did it today.

Today, it seemed as if
my world came to an end.
Today, I stopped believing,
hoping, and wishing.
Today, I felt a pain
that I wouldn't wish on my worst enemy.
Today was the worst day of my life.

Today, I cried non-stop.
Today, I felt my heart drop.
Today, I blamed myself, my friends, my family,
and I even blamed God.
Today, I did what a lot of black mamas
have had to do (unfortunately).
Today, I buried my son!

YESTERDAY'S DREAMER

Yesterday your problems were few,
and your pleasures were many.
Yesterday you had dreams,
but today you don't have any.

Yesterday you believed
your dreams would come true.
But today you realize
those dreams weren't for you.

Yesterday your future
seemed very bright.
But today's complications
have turned out the light.

Yesterday your life
was better in every way.
But all that is behind now,
because that was yesterday.

OUR WORLD TODAY

It seems to me
in this day and time,
evil rules our hearts and minds.

Our world today
is in a sad situation.
Selfishness and greed
are ruining our nation.

No one has the time
to lend a helping hand.
No one gives a damn
about his fellowman.

Our children today
are totally neglected.
Our elderly today
are very disrespected.

Who can we turn to?
Who can we trust?
This world is full of corruption,
and filled with disgust.

Our world today
is in a sad situation.
Evil rules this whole damn nation!

FAMILY CYCLES

There are cycles in our families
reoccurring extremely fast.
Children are making the same mistakes
their parents made in the past.

A young boy grows up fatherless,
and suffers heartache and pain.
Later he becomes an absent father,
starting this cycle over again.

A teenage girl becomes pregnant
after having sex with her boyfriend.
Thirteen years later,
her daughter continues the family trend.

A father goes to prison for life,
But little did he know,
his son would follow his lead,
and now sits on death row.

A young mother drops out of school,
lacking a high school education.
Unfortunately due to the cycle,
her daughter faces the same situation.

We as parents must realize
children learn from what we do.
And we must not forget that someday,
they will be parents too.

THE WHIE GIRL BLUES

As she looked at me
with her blonde hair and blues eyes;
she said: "What I'm about to say to you
may come as a surprise.
But I haven't always lived
some white girl's charmed life.
My days here on this earth
have been filled with stress and strife.
Up until the age of thirteen,
I thought my name was "Bitch".
And still today when I hear gunfire,
I head straight for the nearest ditch.
And that sorry uncle of mine,
I wish his ass was dead.
The things he used to do to me,
I still can't get out of my head.
At the age of sixteen,
I had to get out on my own.
My mamma put me out of the house,
because she said I was too damn grown.
I've been used, abused,
and tossed to the side.
Many nights I've laid in bed
and did nothing but cried.
I never knew what love was
during my early years.
And the water you see in these blue eyes
are hurtful, painful tears.
So, don't you dare for one minute
think I haven't paid my dues,
because my whole life has been the white girl blues".

YOU'LL NEVER KNOW

Dear Mommy,
You'll never know
who I could have been!
What I could have been!
Or how great I could have been!

You'll never know
the joy I could have given you!
The pleasure I would have brought to you!
Or the love I would have had for you!

Because of your own selfishness;
you'll never know
how wonderful of a life
I could have had!

And unfortunately for me,
neither will I!

Signed: Your aborted child

CHILDHOOD DREAMS

When I was a child
I had big goals, big ideas,
big ambitions, and big dreams...
but then life happened,
and reality set in.

Now as an adult,
I still have big goals, big ideas,
big ambitions, and big dreams...for my child.

BUT MOMMY!

But mommy!
You said you would protect me
from all harm and danger.
And still, you gave me to him
as if I was a stranger.

But mommy!
You said to never let anyone
touch me there.
And still, you allowed him
to put his hand in my underwear.

But mommy!
You said you would never
allow this to happen to me.
And still, you just sat back
and let it be.

But mommy!
You said if this ever did happen,
for me to come to you.
But now I am confused,
and I don't know what to do.

Listen child!
Maybe when you grow up
you'll be able to understand,
there are just some things a woman has to do
in order to keep her man.

ANOTHER BLACK YOUTH TALE

His mother works the night shift,
and his father is unknown.
Thirteen years old,
growing up on his own.

No one to kiss him goodnight,
or give him a hug.
He finds great comfort
in being a thug.

Hanging out with his homies
at all hours of the night.
Kicked out of school
for starting fight after fight.

Doing nothing all day,
while other kids are in school.
With time on his hands,
he decides to act a damn fool.

Walks into a store
with a gun in hand.
"Give me all the money!"
He shouts in demand.

But little does he know,
the clerk has a gun on the scene.
One shot to the head,
and he never sees fourteen.

OUTSIDE MY WINDOW

Outside my window,
I watch from day to day.
I see so many lives
slowly wasting away.

I see a street whore
trying to make fast money.
Her life is a joke,
but the joke ain't funny.

I see young black males
looking like damn fools,
with their pants off their asses,
thinking that shit is cool.

I see a teenage girl
laughing with another.
Only thirteen years old,
and already an unfit mother.

I see a homeless man
in search of food to eat.
I see a drunken old woman
who has given in to defeat.

Outside my window,
I watch from day to day.
I see so many lives
slowly slipping away.

PART 5

PRESSURE, PRIDE, AND PAIN

THAT DAY

She will never forget that day
the army chaplain knocked on her door.
Right away she knew
she wouldn't see him anymore.

The chaplain said he died a hero,
and served his country with pride.
But still the pain in her heart
made her wish she had died.

She felt a deep hurt
that she had never felt before.
On her life she felt as if someone
had just slammed the door.

Her nights were sleepless,
and her days were long.
For the child he never met,
she tried to be strong.

A major part of her life
had suddenly been taken away.
Nothing could have prepared her
for "That day".

ROLE REVERSAL

She rolled over in bed,
only to find he wasn't there.
She got up and ran to the window,
wearing nothing but her underwear.

She looked out of the window,
with tears pouring down her face.
The man she loved so much
was gone without a trace.

She called out his name,
only to get a returned silence.
She began to remember the abuse
and all the drunken violence.

She remembered the bruises,
the black eyes, and busted lips.
She remembered the late night,
embarrassing hospital trips.

It all came back to her.
She remembered why she was alone.
Damn! She said to herself.
I'm the reason he's gone.

She remembered him leaving,
and slamming the door.
The last thing he said was...
"I can't take your abuse anymore!"

AM I?

Am I your friend
or your foe?
If you no longer love me,
please let me know!

Am I your woman
or your bitch?
Sometimes it's hard to tell
which is which.

Are we together
or apart?
Please stop playing games
with my heart.

Either you want me,
or you don't.
Please answer me,
Am I the one you want?

DILEMMA #1 (What Should I Do?)

He keeps on pressuring me,
and I don't know what to do!
I'm really not ready for this,
but I don't want him to leave me
for one of those other girls.
He said if I prove my love to him,
he will love me forever.
All of our friends are doing it.
So, why shouldn't we?
But I'm scared! I'm too young for this!
And there are so many girls in my school
who are pregnant, or already mothers.
And I'm just in junior high!
I don't want to be one of those girls.
I have so much going for me right now.
I wish I could talk to my mother about this,
but I already know what she would say.
And daddy, well that's out of the question!
I better decide quick because he's on the way over,
and my parents will be gone for hours.

What should I do?
What should I do?
What should I do?

Well, there's the door bell...

DILEMMA #2 (How Do I Tell Them?)

I'm only fourteen years old!
How did I get myself in this mess?
Should I keep this life that lives inside me?
If so, How do I tell my parents?
Daddy is going to be so pissed off with me,
and mamma is going to be very disappointed
in her baby girl.
How will I take care of a child? I'm just a child myself!
It's obvious I can't take care of myself, if so,
I wouldn't be in this situation (damn, I was so stupid!).
I shouldn't have ever did it. I knew better!
I know that sorry ass ex-boyfriend of mine won't help.
He says the baby ain't his anyway.
And I know it is, because he's the only one I've ever been
with in that way. And he knows that too!
At least I know this child will love me (unlike other people).
I owe it to this child to allow it to have a chance at life,
even if it means ruining my own.
How can I do the right thing when I don't know what the
right thing is?
I know people will talk about me behind my back, and say
ugly things about me. I know this because I used to do the
same thing to other girls in this situation. (I guess this is what
my parents mean when they say, the shoe is on the other
foot). Now I'll be the new gossip in school.

My parents have always been there for me, but will they be
there this time? I guess I'll find out soon enough.
But first I'll go to the doctor and hear what he says.

DILEMMA #3 (How Could This Be?)

Oh, my God!
How could this be?
The doctor just told me
I have HIV.
Oh, no! This can't be true!
I never thought this would happen to me!
I'm not supposed to have HIV.
I'm too young for this! Please Lord,
don't let this be! How could You do this to me?
I only had sex once! We used protection! At least
I thought we did (he said he had a condom on).
I was gonna go to my high school prom one day!
I was gonna go to college!
I was even hoping to get married one day!
But now, my whole life has changed!
All because I made one bad decision!
Damn, I was stupid! Stupid! Stupid!
I wish I could take it all back.
I wish I could do it all over again! Because
this time I would say NO!
Ain't no boy worth all this!

Wait a minute... he gave it to me!
I wonder if he even knows he has it.
Well, I'll tell him, and then I'm gonna kill him!

What about the baby? Are we both doomed?
What will my parents say about this?

DILEMMA #4 (Daddy's Revenge)

Damn, I'm gonna kill'em!
I gonna kill'em right now!
How dare he do this to my baby!
It's bad enough he got her pregnant,
but now H-I-V!
I'm gonna kill'em!
I should have never let her mama talk me
into letting her date so soon (I should kill her ass too!)
I never thought this would happen to my baby!
No!
No!
No!
It can't be true! It just can't be!
I'm going over to that school right now.
I'm gonna kill'em right there on the spot.
He thinks he's some big deal!
Well, we will just see about that!
He got the nerve to say the baby ain't his, well let's
see if this HIV is his. Let's see if he claims that,
because it sure as hell will claim him.
Damn, little sneaky bastard!
He don't have to worry about AIDS taking his life,
because I'm gonna take it before AIDS has a chance.

There he is right there!
Let me pull this car over now.
Hey! Hey! Don't run! Come here you!

NOT ANOTHER DAY

He woke up that morning,
and jumped out of bed.
Sweet thoughts of her
filled his head.

He ran down stairs,
hoping to see her face.
But when he arrived,
she was not in place.

He called out her name,
but only silence replied.
He searched and searched,
while like a baby he cried.

He looked out of the window
with his eyes full of tears.
He then realized she had been dead
for over two years.

He came back to reality,
and calmed himself down.
He remembered the day
he helplessly watched her drown.

He went down to the river,
and asked God to forgive his sin.
He then closed his eyes
and jumped right in.

HOW MANY?

Woman! Why are you allowing yourself
to be treated in such a terrible way?
Is your love for him stronger than
the love you have for yourself?

Why are you allowing this man
to beat you in front of your child?
How could he possibly have any respect for you
as a woman, as a mother, or a person?

How many times are you going to call the police,
only to tell them everything is alright when they arrive?
How many lies are you going to tell your friends,
while trying to explain the bruises on your face?

How many times are you going to allow him to apologize,
only for him to do it again as soon as he gets angry?
How many days are you going to miss out of work
while waiting for the swelling to go down?

How many trips to the emergency room
will it take for you to realize that your relationship
with this man is not healthy for you?
Nor is it a good example to set for your daughter?

The big question is:
HOW MANY?
How many more beatings are you going to take
before you decide enough is enough?

PRESSURE, PRIDE, AND PAIN

John was a proud man,
with a small family to feed.
He took great pride
in providing for their needs.

John worked hard
for his wife and baby boy.
Taking care of them both
gave John so much joy.

But then one day,
all of sudden, out of the blue!
John lost his job,
and his wife left him too!

John was a broken man,
his whole world had been destroyed.
He couldn't live without his family,
nor could he take being unemployed.

John couldn't sleep at night,
he just cried, cried, and cried.
The pressure of losing everything
was building up inside.

John went on a rampage,
shooting everything in sight.
After killing his small family,
he then turned out his own light.

WHAT AM I TO BE?

My mom is a sorry crack-head,
and my dad is a drunken dead-beat.
They tell me I'm gonna be nothing,
so I may as well face defeat.

My brother is already in jail,
and my sister is a two dollar whore.
And when they look at me,
they say I'll be nothing more.

They all laugh in my face,
and call me out my name.
They say when I look in the mirror,
I should see nothing but shame.

I really must admit,
I have a fucked-up family tree.
With a family like this,
what am I to be?

Can I beat the odds?
Or will I just be the same?
Will I rise above this?
Or will I carry on the family name?

I ask myself so often,
what am I to be?
I guess the answer to the question
is totally up to me.

HOUSE NIGGER/FIELD NIGGER

Back in the day,
when the black man was a slave,
house nigger and field nigger
were the titles the master gave.

The field nigger worked the fields;
picking cotton and bailing hay,
While the house nigger worked the master;
trying to get favors his own way.

The field niggers had unity,
They always worked together.
But the house niggers only concerns
were to make their lives better.

Because the house nigger believed
the field nigger was a threat,
he became the worst enemy
the field nigger ever met.

If the field nigger had a plan
to escape from his master,
there was that house nigger
causing the plan to be a disaster.

One of the major issues
holding back the black race,
is that "house nigger attitude"
that we have to face.

Peace
&
Blessings

ABOUT THE AUTHOR

Pierre D. Perry is a North Carolina native, and the proud father of two beautiful daughters. He is a graduate of Franklinton High School, and a U.S. Navy veteran. Perry is the author of seven books of poetry, and the founder of PDP Publishing and 4USBOOKS. He has been employed with the North Carolina Department of Public Safety for over 23 years (formerly known as the North Carolina Department of Corrections). To contact Pierre for poetry readings or book signings please email him at pierredperry65@yahoo.com

Pierre D. Perry currently resides in Henderson, North Carolina, where he is working on his net book.